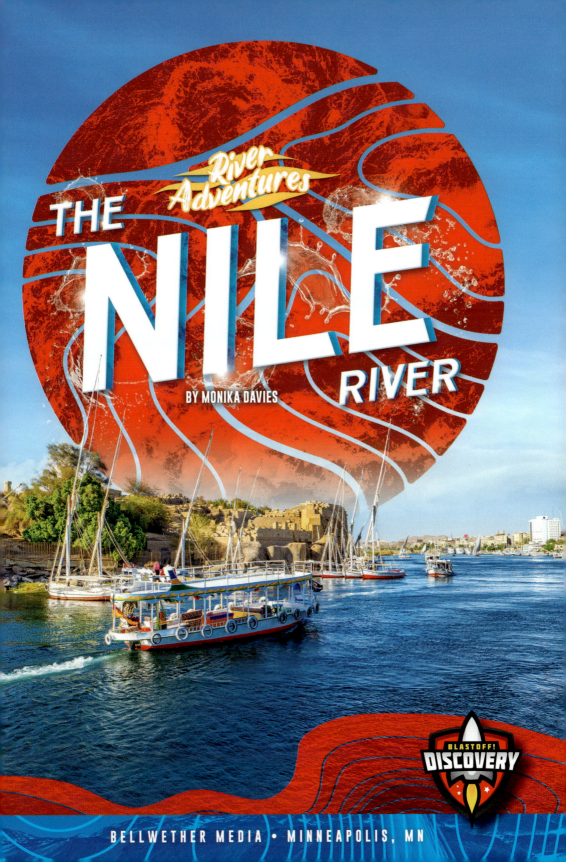

This edition first published in 2025 by Bellwether Media, Inc.

No part of this publication may be reproduced in whole or in part without written permission of the publisher. For information regarding permission, write to Bellwether Media, Inc., Attention: Permissions Department, 6012 Blue Circle Drive, Minnetonka, MN 55343.

Library of Congress Cataloging-in-Publication Data

Names: Davies, Monika, author.
Title: The Nile River / by Monika Davies.
Description: Minneapolis, MN : Bellwether Media, 2025. | Series: Blastoff! Discovery: River adventures | Includes bibliographical references and index. | Audience: Ages 7-13 | Audience: Grades 4-6 | Summary: "Engaging images accompany information about the Nile River. The combination of high-interest subject matter and narrative text is intended for students in grades 3 through 8"– Provided by publisher.
Identifiers: LCCN 2024016562 (print) | LCCN 2024016563 (ebook) | ISBN 9798893040005 (library binding) | ISBN 9781644879320 (ebook)
Subjects: LCSH: Nile River–Juvenile literature.
Classification: LCC DT115 .D297 2025 (print) | LCC DT115 (ebook) | DDC 962–dc23/eng/20240513
LC record available at https://lccn.loc.gov/2024016562
LC ebook record available at https://lccn.loc.gov/2024016563

Text copyright © 2025 by Bellwether Media, Inc. BLASTOFF! DISCOVERY and associated logos are trademarks and/or registered trademarks of Bellwether Media, Inc. Bellwether Media is a division of Chrysalis Education Group.

Editor: Rachael Barnes   Designer: Brittany McIntosh

Printed in the United States of America, North Mankato, MN.

Table of Contents

Two Banks, One River	4
Geography	6
Plants and Animals	12
Human History	16
The River Today	22
Protecting the River	26
Glossary	30
To Learn More	31
Index	32

TWO BANKS, ONE RIVER

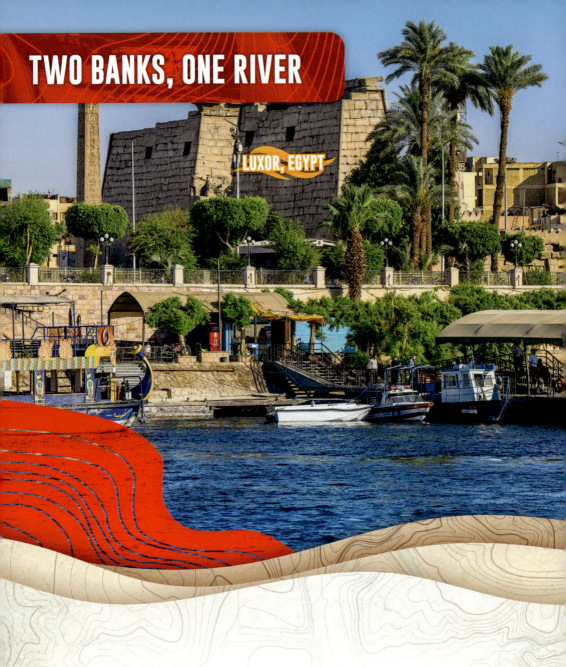

LUXOR, EGYPT

It is a busy morning in Luxor, Egypt. As the sun rises, the reflection of the Temples of Luxor sparkles in the Nile River. The sandstone temples stand on the east bank. Around the temples, people hurry to and from work. Some locals board ferries to cross the river. Others paddle boats to large cruise ships. They sell items to curious travelers.

Later, a group enjoys the sunset from their ship. They watch shadows fall on the farms and ancient **tombs** that cover the river's west bank. Egrets fly overhead. The ship travels upstream as night falls on the Nile River.

GEOGRAPHY

LAKE VICTORIA IN KENYA

The majestic Nile River crosses through eastern Africa. The 4,132-mile- (6,650-kilometer-) long river weaves its way from south to north through 11 countries. The Nile appears to have no single **source**. Instead, the river's waters come from multiple rivers that start in Burundi and Rwanda. The Kagera River is the Nile's southernmost source.

These rivers feed Lake Victoria, the largest lake in Africa. This vast but shallow lake spreads into parts of Tanzania, Uganda, and Kenya. The Nile begins its journey from there.

The Nile flows from the north side of Lake Victoria. Starting near Jinja, Uganda, the Nile flows through lakes and swamps. After passing through Lake Albert, the river next reaches South Sudan and travels through tight valleys. The river spreads out as it moves through the Al-Sudd region. Long grasses grow in these **wetlands**.

JINJA

LAKE ALBERT IN UGANDA

THE MOUNTAIN NILE

In South Sudan, there is a stretch of the Nile called the Mountain Nile. It flows from Nimule to Juba and feeds the White Nile River.

SOUTH SUDAN

From northern South Sudan, the river runs through wide valleys into central Sudan. This section is called the White Nile. It is one of the river's major **tributaries**. Another is the Blue Nile. It rushes down from the Ethiopian **Plateau**.

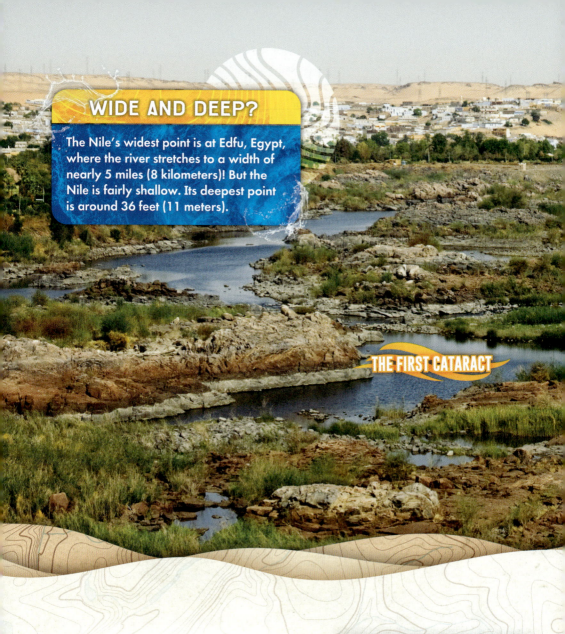

WIDE AND DEEP?

The Nile's widest point is at Edfu, Egypt, where the river stretches to a width of nearly 5 miles (8 kilometers)! But the Nile is fairly shallow. Its deepest point is around 36 feet (11 meters).

THE FIRST CATARACT

The White Nile and Blue Nile meet in central Sudan. Their **confluence** is close to Khartoum, Sudan. Downstream, another big tributary called the Atbara River joins the Nile.

CONFLUENCE NEAR KHARTOUM

The Nile continues north through the Sahara Desert. It then flows through the **Cataracts** of the Nile. These shallow and dangerous parts of the river have powerful **rapids**. Boulders and stones stick out of the riverbed to form six cataracts. The Nile then courses into Lake Nasser. As the river nears Cairo, Egypt, it expands into a **delta**. The Nile funnels into two **channels**. They empty into the river's **mouth** at the Mediterranean Sea.

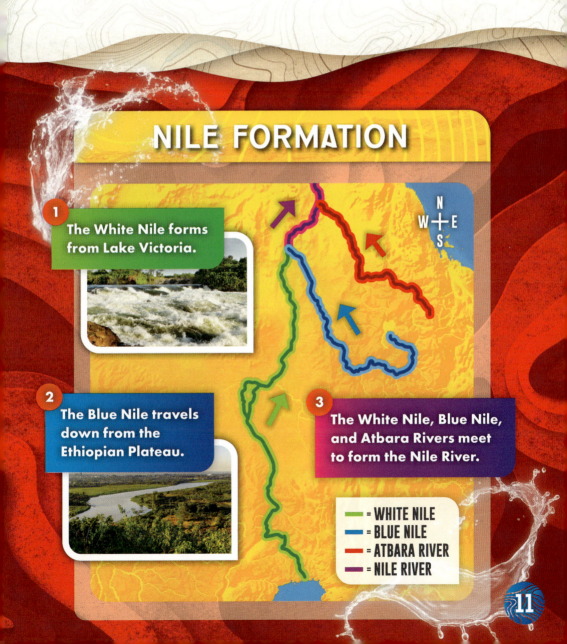

NILE FORMATION

1. The White Nile forms from Lake Victoria.
2. The Blue Nile travels down from the Ethiopian Plateau.
3. The White Nile, Blue Nile, and Atbara Rivers meet to form the Nile River.

— = WHITE NILE
— = BLUE NILE
— = ATBARA RIVER
— = NILE RIVER

PLANTS AND ANIMALS

GELADA

Many plants and animals depend on this river system. Shoebills watch for catfish near Lake Victoria. Along the Blue Nile, gelada graze on mountain plants. Thick, green forests flourish near the river in southwestern Ethiopia. Bamboo and banana plants grow tall.

In the Al-Sudd wetlands, tall papyrus, reeds, and grasses sway in the wind. Nile lechwes wander shallow waters, chewing on grasses. Nile crocodiles wait for prey. African elephants wade through the wetlands. Hippos sleep on the riverbanks.

PAPYRUS

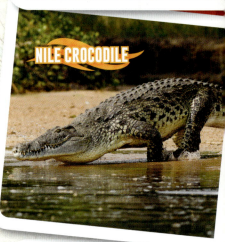
NILE CROCODILE

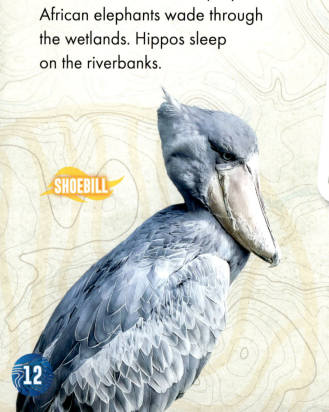
SHOEBILL

HIPPO

NILE LECHWE

Life Span: around 10 years
Status: endangered

Nile lechwe range =

| LEAST CONCERN | NEAR THREATENED | VULNERABLE | ENDANGERED | CRITICALLY ENDANGERED | EXTINCT IN THE WILD | EXTINCT |

Acacias are among the few trees that grow in the dry desert around the Nile. Many reptiles in the area rely on the Nile to survive. Monitor lizards sunbathe on rocks. Around 30 types of snakes slither by the river. Softshell turtles make their homes on the river's muddy bottom.

NILE MONITOR LIZARD

ACACIA TREES

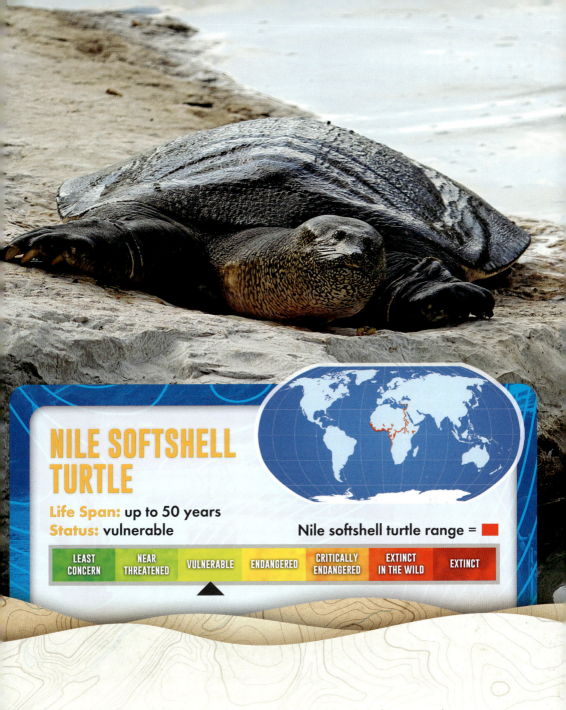

NILE SOFTSHELL TURTLE

Life Span: up to 50 years
Status: vulnerable

Nile softshell turtle range =

| LEAST CONCERN | NEAR THREATENED | VULNERABLE | ENDANGERED | CRITICALLY ENDANGERED | EXTINCT IN THE WILD | EXTINCT |

Many different fish swim in the Nile. Nile perches use their wide mouths to gobble up insects and other fish. Tigerfish snap up prey with their sharp teeth. Lungfish swish past and use their back limbs to push off rocks!

HUMAN HISTORY

Different groups throughout history have depended on the Nile River. Around 5000 BCE, people began to move from the Sahara toward the river. They moved into Nubia, or modern-day Sudan. People began to fish and farm. **Settlements** grew into the ancient kingdom of Kush.

The Kush kingdom used the Nile as a trade route. Ships carried gold, ivory, oils, and other fine goods. Around 3000 BCE, a united Egyptian **civilization** quickly grew next to the Nile River. They built grand pyramids, temples, and tombs. They fought for control of the river and the surrounding land. The Egyptians eventually took over Nubia and much of the Nile.

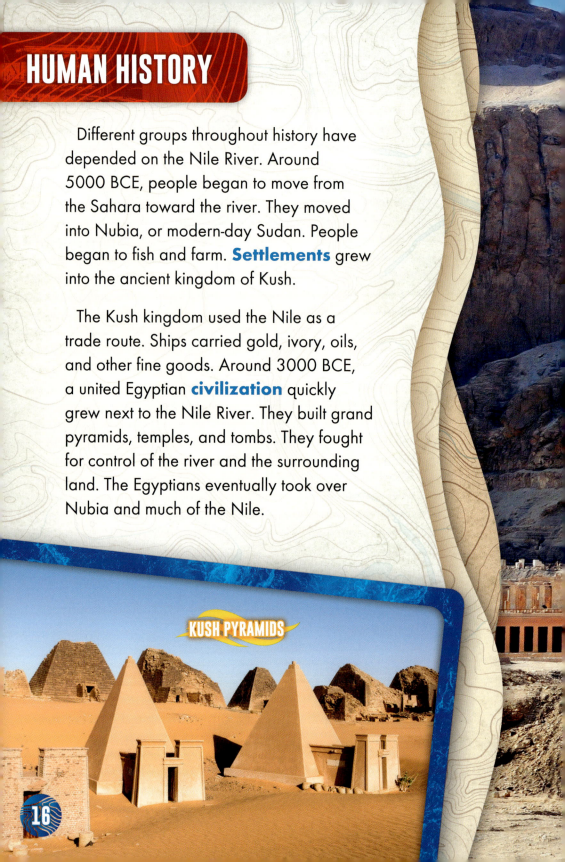

KUSH PYRAMIDS

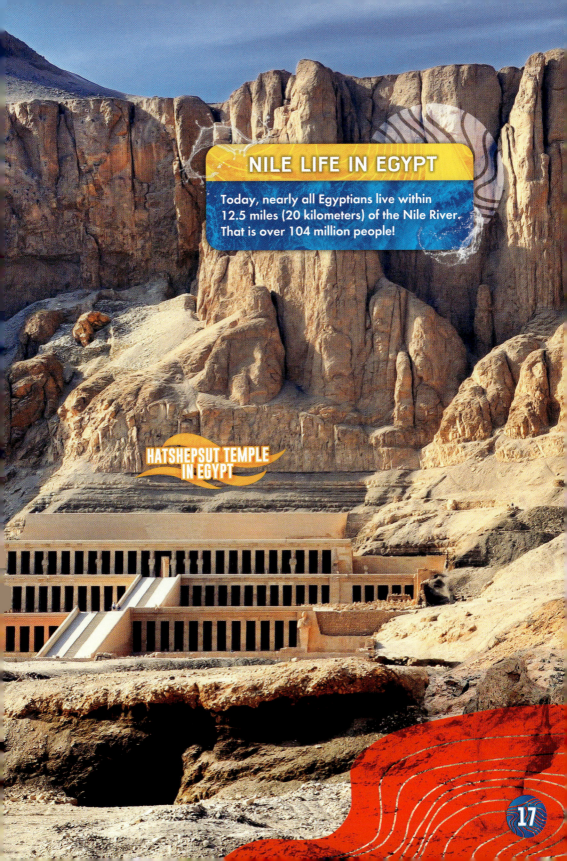

NILE LIFE IN EGYPT

Today, nearly all Egyptians live within 12.5 miles (20 kilometers) of the Nile River. That is over 104 million people!

HATSHEPSUT TEMPLE IN EGYPT

IRRIGATION SYSTEM

BLACK SHORELINE

Ancient Egyptians called the river *Ar* or *Aur*. This means "black." It described the color of the silt the river carried in late summer.

Egyptian civilization learned to live with the river. Reed and wood boats allowed people to easily travel and move building supplies. Fishermen brought in huge catches. Fish from the Nile were a major source of food and trade.

Egyptians also tracked the river's annual flooding. Every year from about September to January, the Nile overflowed and left behind **silt**. The rich soil this created made the land ideal for farming. Egyptians built an **irrigation** system to collect floodwater. They used the Nile's floodwater to grow wheat and flax farther away from the river.

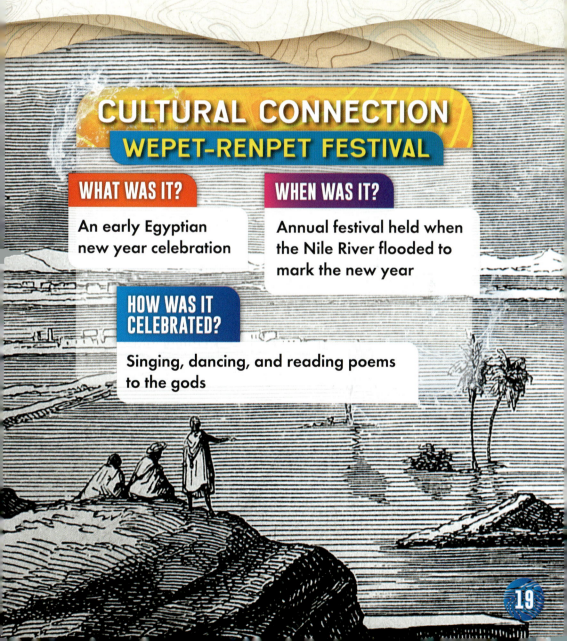

CULTURAL CONNECTION
WEPET-RENPET FESTIVAL

WHAT WAS IT?
An early Egyptian new year celebration

WHEN WAS IT?
Annual festival held when the Nile River flooded to mark the new year

HOW WAS IT CELEBRATED?
Singing, dancing, and reading poems to the gods

Greek explorers traveled upstream between 457 and 25 BCE. They recorded the path of the river and major landmarks. In 1618, Spaniard Pedro Páez discovered the source of the Blue Nile. Scottish explorer James Bruce found the spring again in 1770. European interest in the Nile grew.

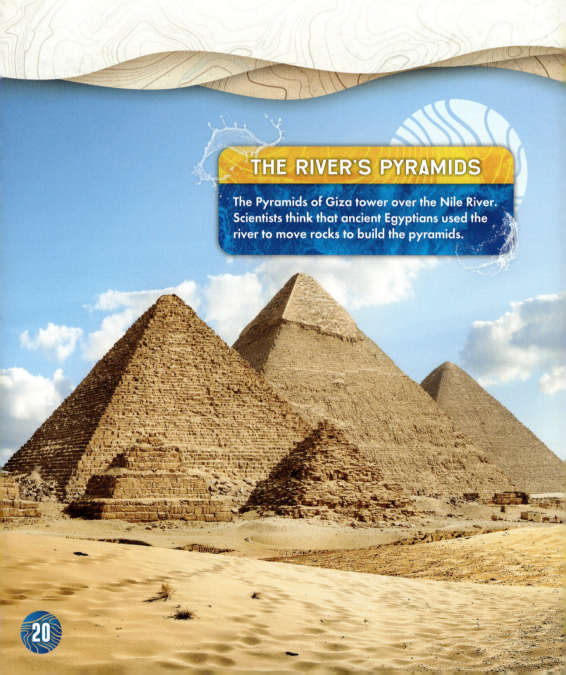

THE RIVER'S PYRAMIDS

The Pyramids of Giza tower over the Nile River. Scientists think that ancient Egyptians used the river to move rocks to build the pyramids.

NILE RIVER TIMELINE

AROUND 3000 BCE
A united Egyptian civilization grows along the banks of the Nile

457 TO 25 BCE
Several Greek explorers travel on the Nile, recording its path and landmarks

1618 CE
Pedro Páez discovers the source of the Blue Nile

1999
The Nile Basin Initiative is launched to care for the river

2023
The Grand Ethiopian Renaissance Dam opens

    In 1858, Englishman John Hanning Speke sought the source of the Nile. He sailed to Lake Victoria and named it after the queen of his homeland. Over the years, people built structures to control the Nile's flow. In 1902, the first major dam opened at Aswan, Egypt. In 1970, Aswan High Dam opened a few miles away.

THE RIVER TODAY

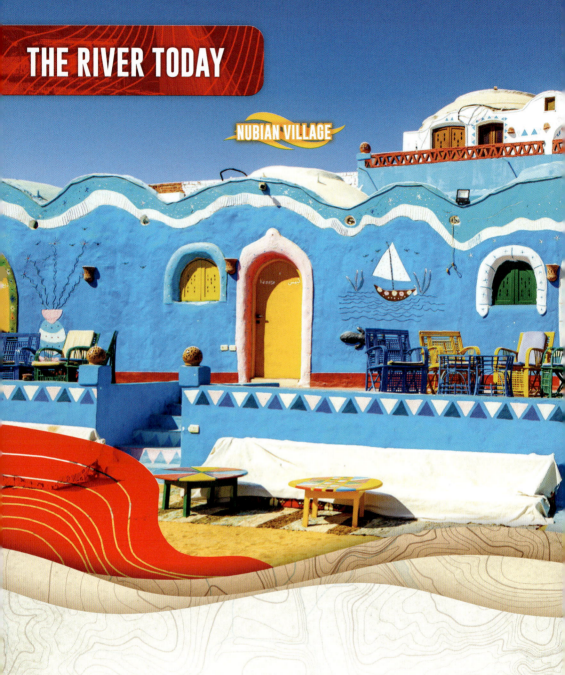

NUBIAN VILLAGE

Today, the Nile flows past both historical and modern-day structures. Bustling cities, like Cairo and Aswan, rise next to the Nile. Many people visit historic Luxor and colorful Nubian villages along the river.

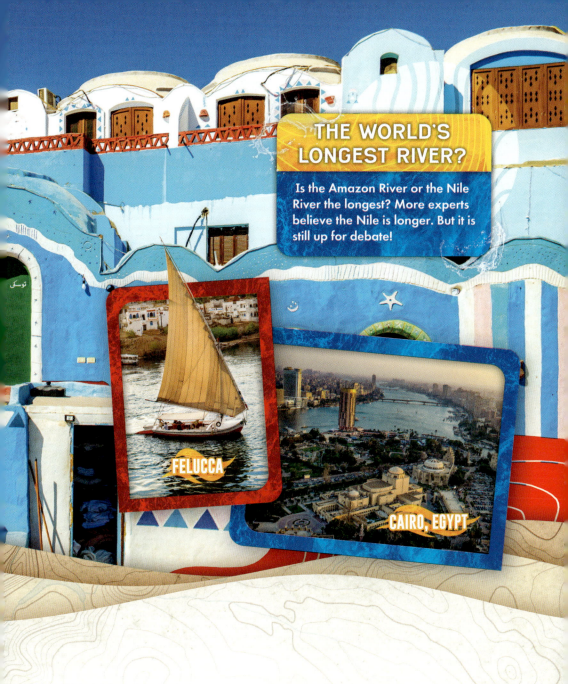

THE WORLD'S LONGEST RIVER?

Is the Amazon River or the Nile River the longest? More experts believe the Nile is longer. But it is still up for debate!

FELUCCA

CAIRO, EGYPT

   The Nile also continues to serve as a key waterway. Some people use it to travel between cities. Others use it as a trade route from Africa to many European ports. People fish in the Nile's waters. Many people sail the river on **traditional** sailboats, like feluccas.

ASWAN HIGH DAM

The Nile continues to support and sustain life. Around 280 million people depend on the river. Farmers still grow crops in the rich soil that borders the Nile. Water from the river irrigates crops. Many dams operating along the river help this process.

The Aswan High Dam continues to control flooding. The dam can hold back floodwaters until it is time to water crops. It also produces **hydropower**. Over the last few decades, over 25 hydropower dams were built along the river and its major tributaries. The Grand Ethiopian Renaissance Dam (GERD) is one of the largest projects.

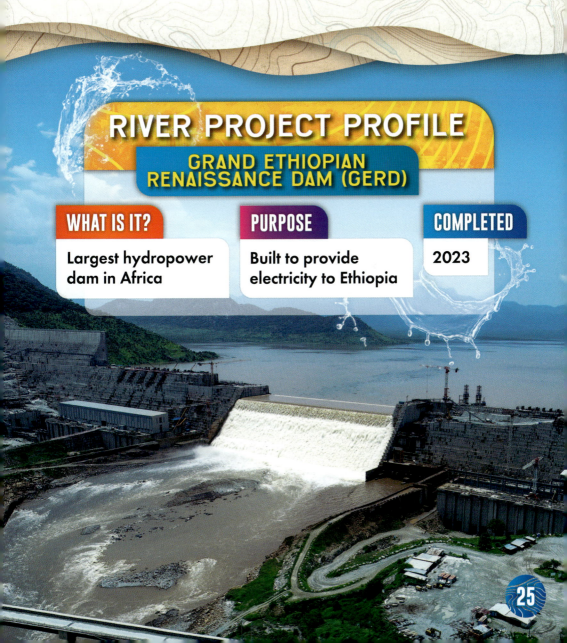

RIVER PROJECT PROFILE
GRAND ETHIOPIAN RENAISSANCE DAM (GERD)

WHAT IS IT?
Largest hydropower dam in Africa

PURPOSE
Built to provide electricity to Ethiopia

COMPLETED
2023

PROTECTING THE RIVER

The Nile has grown more polluted over the years. Floods helped flush out waste in the water. But there are fewer floods as dams take over the Nile. Waste builds up over time.

Researchers have found heavy metals at the bottom of the river, like cadmium and nickel. The heavy metals poison animals that swim the waters. Parts of the river have metal levels that are also unsafe for humans. Some of this damage might be impossible to reverse.

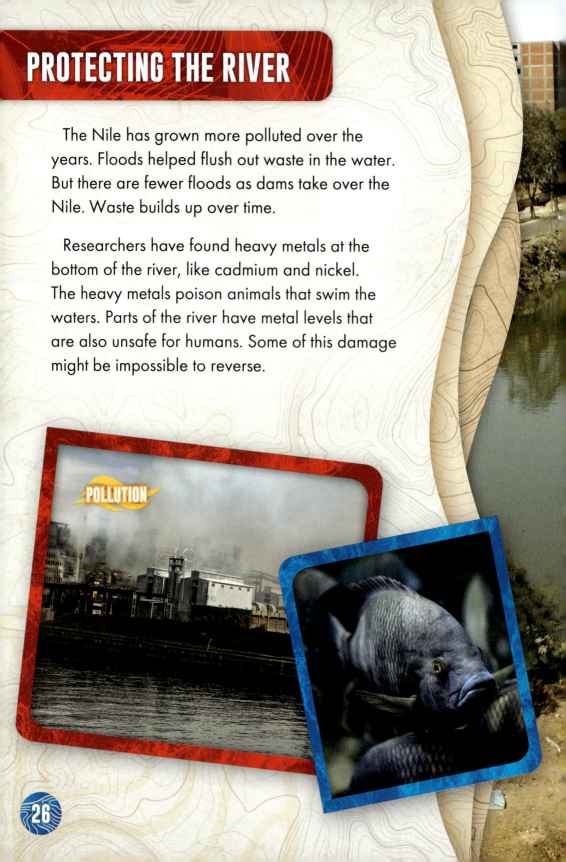

POLLUTION

Since 1999, the Nile Basin Initiative has worked to protect the river. This group of countries is addressing concerns around water security. Another goal of theirs is to manage the impact of **climate change** on the river. Other organizations are also lending a hand. Some host cleaning events to remove plastic waste from the river.

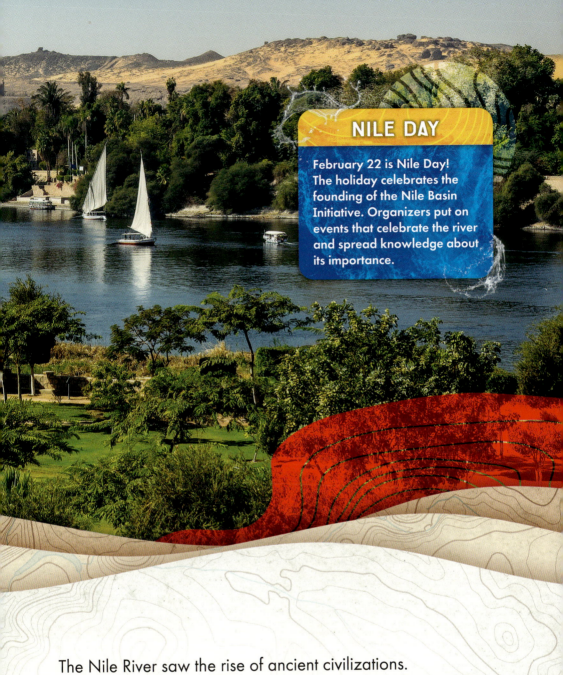

NILE DAY

February 22 is Nile Day! The holiday celebrates the founding of the Nile Basin Initiative. Organizers put on events that celebrate the river and spread knowledge about its importance.

The Nile River saw the rise of ancient civilizations. The river stretches through multiple countries, touching the lives of many. People are working together to help the magnificent Nile continue to stand the test of time.

GLOSSARY

cataracts—shallow areas of a river that are rocky and dangerous to move through

channels—paths where water flows; channels often connect rivers to larger bodies of water.

civilization—a highly developed, organized society

climate change—a human-caused change to Earth's weather due to warming temperatures

confluence—the place where two rivers meet

delta—a land area that forms where a river flows into a large body of water

hydropower—the energy created by moving water

irrigation—related to the act or process of supplying water to an area

mouth—the place where a river empties into a larger body of water

plateau—a flat, raised area of land

rapids—parts of a river where the water flows very fast, often over rocks

settlements—places that people move to and make their home

silt—tiny pieces of dirt, rock, and other materials that can be left behind by moving water

source—the beginning of a river

tombs—buildings above ground that house dead bodies

traditional—related to customs, ideas, or beliefs handed down from one generation to the next

tributaries—rivers and streams that flow into a larger stream, river, or lake

wetlands—areas of land that are covered with low levels of water for most of the year

TO LEARN MORE

AT THE LIBRARY

Hudak, Heather C. *Pathways through Africa*. New York, N.Y.: Crabtree Publishing Company, 2020.

Jopp, Kelsey. *Africa*. Lake Elmo, Minn.: Focus Readers, 2020.

Oachs, Emily Rose. *Ancient Egypt*. Minneapolis, Minn.: Bellwether Media, 2020.

ON THE WEB

FACTSURFER

Factsurfer.com gives you a safe, fun way to find more information.

1. Go to www.factsurfer.com.

2. Enter "Nile River" into the search box and click 🔍.

3. Select your book cover to see a list of related content.

INDEX

Africa, 6, 7, 23
Al-Sudd, 8, 12
Aswan, Egypt, 21, 22
Blue Nile, 9, 10, 12, 20
boats, 4, 5, 16, 18, 23
Bruce, James, 20
Cairo, Egypt, 11, 22, 23
Cataracts of the Nile, 10, 11
climate change, 28
confluence, 10
countries, 4, 6, 7, 8, 9, 10, 11, 12, 16, 17, 28, 29
cultural connection, 19
dams, 21, 24, 25, 26
delta, 11
Edfu, Egypt, 10
flooding, 19, 25, 26
formation, 11
Grand Ethiopian Renaissance Dam, 25
history, 16, 18, 19, 20, 21, 22, 25, 28, 29
irrigation system, 18, 19, 24
Jinja, Uganda, 8
Khartoum, Sudan, 10
lakes, 6, 7, 8, 11, 12, 21

Luxor, Egypt, 4, 22
map, 7
Mediterranean Sea, 11
Mountain Nile, 9
mouth, 11
name, 18
Nile Basin Initiative, 28, 29
Nile Day, 29
Páez, Pedro, 20
people, 4, 5, 16, 17, 18, 19, 20, 21, 22, 23, 24, 26, 29
pollution, 26
pyramids, 16, 20
river project profile, 25
Sahara Desert, 11, 14, 16
size, 6, 10, 23
source, 6, 20, 21
Speke, John Hanning, 21
Temples of Luxor, 4
timeline, 21
trade, 16, 18, 23
tributaries, 9, 10, 12, 20, 25
Wepet-Renpet Festival, 19
White Nile, 9, 10
wildlife, 5, 8, 12, 13, 14, 15, 18, 26

The images in this book are reproduced through the courtesy of: givaga, front cover, pp. 20, 23 (right); HQ-GRAPHICS, p. 3; Ivan Sebborn/ Alamy, pp. 4-5; Ismael Khalifa/ Alamy, p. 5; Stefan Haider, p. 6; Tatsiana Hendzel, p. 8 (top); Oleg Znamenskiy, pp. 8 (bottom), 12 (papyrus); Ville Palonen/ Alamy, p. 9; dbtravel/ Alamy, p. 10 (top); mtcurado/ Getty Images, p. 10 (bottom); Dmitry Pichugin, p. 11 (top); Marisha_SL, p. 11 (bottom); ibrahim altaee, p. 12 (shoebill); Torsten Pursche, p. 12 (gelada); diegooscar01, p. 12 (Nile crocodile); John Carnemolla, p. 12 (hippo); Ernie Janes/ Alamy, p. 13; MattiaATH, p. 14 (top); Tunde Gaspar, p. 14 (bottom); Ben Rokhlenko, p. 15; Hussain Warraich, p. 16; Maxal Tamor, pp. 16-17; Independent Picture Service/ Alamy, p. 18; Colin Waters/ Alamy, p. 19; Matyas Rehak, p. 21 (top); Grentidez/ Wikipedia, p. 21 (bottom); Elizaveta Larionova/ Alamy, pp. 22-23; AlexAnton, p. 23 (left); remon fayez, p. 24; dpa picture alliance/ Alamy, p. 25; Terence Waeland/ Alamy, p. 26 (left); Captain Wang, p. 26 (right); Alan Gignoux/ Alamy, pp. 26-27; Delpixel, pp. 28-29; Alexander Cher, p. 31.